D1029034

First Facts®

Underground Safari

GRUBS, BUGS, AND WORMS
INVERTEBRATES OF THE UNDERGROUND

by Jody Sullivan Rake

Consultant:
Kyle Wickings, PhD
Assistant Professor, Department of Entomology
Cornell University
Ithaca, New York

CAPSTONE PRESS
a capstone imprint

First Facts are published by Capstone Press,
1710 Roe Crest Drive, North Mankato, Minnesota 56003
www.capstonepub.com

Copyright © 2016 by Capstone Press, a Capstone imprint. All rights reserved. No part of this publication may be reproduced in whole or in part, or stored in a retrieval system, or transmitted in any form or by any means, electronic, mechanical, photocopying, recording, or otherwise, without written permission of the publisher.

Library of Congress Cataloging-in-Publication Data
Rake, Jody Sullivan, author.
  Grubs, bugs, and worms : invertebrates of the underground / by Jody Sullivan Rake.
      pages cm. — (Underground safari)
  Summary: "Teaches readers about invertebrates that live underground, including insects, spiders, and worms"—Provided by publisher.
  Includes bibliographical references and index.
  ISBN 978-1-4914-5061-1 (library binding)
  ISBN 978-1-4914-5091-8 (ebook pdf)
1. Insects—Juvenile literature. 2. Worms—Juvenile literature. 3. Invertebrates—Juvenile literature. I. Title. II. Series: Rake, Jody Sullivan. Underground safari.
  QL467.2.R345 2015
  595.7—dc23
                        2015003665

Editorial Credits
Abby Colich, editor; Heidi Thompson, designer; Jo Miller, media researcher; Katy LaVigne, production specialist

Photo Credits
Corbis: Visuals Unlimited/Alex Wild, 15; James P. Rowan, 8, 11, 16, 17, 19; Nature Picture Library: Dietmer Nill, 5, Hans Christoph Kappel, 21; Newscom: imago stock & people, 13; Shutterstock: Andrey Pavlov, 3 (left), Anest, 3 (right), D. Jucharski K. Kucharska, cover (right), 7, Gucio_55, 9, J. Helgason, cover, 1 (background), Pakhnyushchy, cover (left), schankz, 14, Steve Byland, cover (middle)

Design Elements
Shutterstock: Hal_P, LudmilaM

Printed in China by Nordica
0415/CA21500544
042015   008845NORDF15

TABLE OF CONTENTS

DISHING THE DIRT

The ground beneath your feet is full of life! Thousands of animal *species* live in the dirt below. Many of these animals are bugs and other *invertebrates*—animals without backbones. These invertebrates can live all or part of their lives underground. These creatures have important jobs in nature.

species—a group of creatures that can reproduce with one another

invertebrate—an animal without a backbone

The number of creatures living underground is much higher than those living above ground!

WIGGLY WONDERS

Earthworms wiggle through the dirt in many parts of the world. These creatures are *decomposers*. They eat bits of dead plants and animals. Their waste is full of nutrients that *fertilize* the soil. Many earthworms feed above ground at night. They *burrow* below ground during the day.

DIG IN!

How do earthworms burrow without claws or feet? Their bodies have rows of tiny, hairlike *bristles*. The bristles push earthworms forward through the dirt.

decomposer—a living thing that turns dead things into food for others
fertilize—to make soil rich and healthy
burrow—to dig a tunnel or hole in the ground
bristle—short, stiff hair

▲ earthworm

A GRUB'S LIFE

Many beetle species lay their eggs in the ground. When the eggs hatch, the young don't look like beetles. These *grubs* look like fat worms. The grubs stay underground until they are fully grown. Some beetle species stay near the ground as adults. They burrow in tunnels and eat plants or other insects.

▲ beetle grub

grub—a young insect that looks like a short, white worm

DIG IN!

Beetles are one of the largest groups of animals in the world. More than 350,000 species have been found. That's one-fourth of all known animal species!

▲ adult beetle

17 YEARS IN THE DIRT

Cicadas are flying insects. Like beetles, they lay their eggs in the dirt. One species of cicada *nymph* lives in the soil for 17 years! When the adults come out, clouds of cicadas fill the sky. Adult cicadas only live for a few weeks. They die after laying their eggs.

nymph—a young form of an insect

▼ **cicada nymph**

DIG IN!

The 17-year cicada nymphs eat only tree root sap.

SINGERS IN THE SOIL

Mole crickets chirp like other crickets. You may hear them, but you probably won't see them. These crickets spend most of their lives underground. Mole crickets are built for digging. Their front legs are big, clawed scoopers.

Male mole crickets create burrows shaped like horns. The horn shape makes their chirping louder so more females will hear the chirps.

mole cricket

UNDERGROUND CITIES

Thousands of ant species live below ground. Ants are very *social* bugs. Working together, they build amazing networks of underground tunnels and *chambers*. Ants use the chambers for sleeping, storing food, and laying eggs.

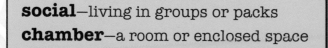

social—living in groups or packs
chamber—a room or enclosed space

▲ **underground ant nest**

DIG IN!

Burrowers are needed in nature. When they move soil around, it helps plants grow.

TUNNELING TERMITES

Termites mostly eat wood and dead plants. Some termites eat parts of buildings, furniture, and books. These termites cause a lot of damage. Many termites live underground. When not nibbling on wood, termites nest in the moist soil. They live in large groups called *colonies*.

DIG IN!

In Australia termites build tall mounds above the ground. These mounds can be 17 feet (5 meters) tall!

colony—a group of the same kind of animal living together

termites

17

HIDEAWAY FOR A HAIRY BEAST

Tarantulas are large, hairy spiders that live underground. Tarantulas don't build webs like aboveground spiders. They dig deep underground burrows and line the walls with *silk* webbing. The webbing keeps out sand and dirt. The tarantulas come out at night to catch their *prey*. They grab the prey with their legs and poison it with *venom*.

silk—a thin but strong thread made by spiders

prey—an animal that is hunted by another animal for food

venom—a liquid poison made by some animals to kill prey

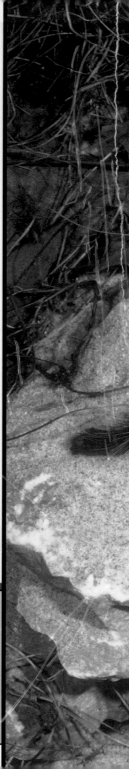

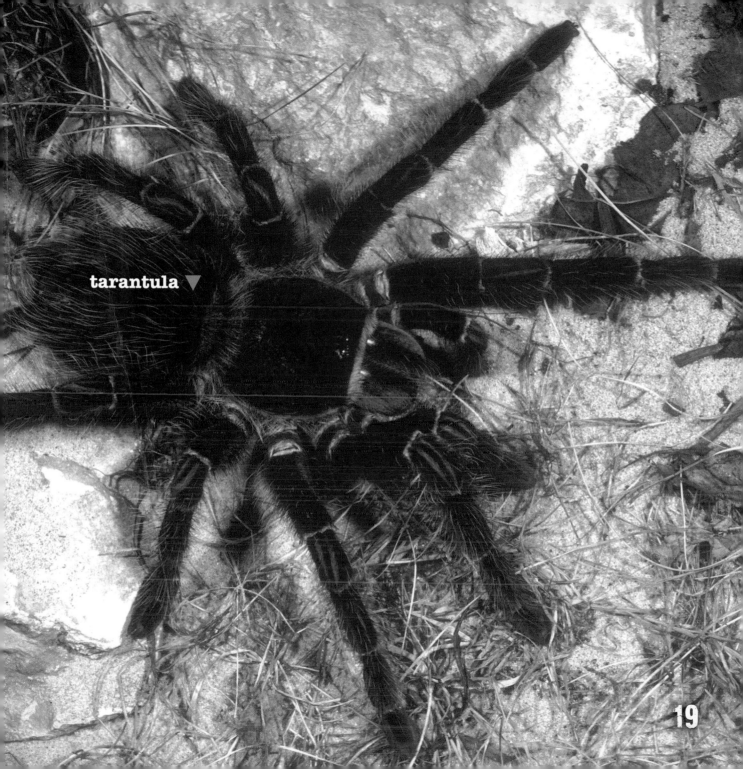

tarantula ▼

19

UNDERGROUND SPIDER TRAP

The trap-door spider has a clever trick. It disguises its burrow opening with a trapdoor. The door is made of dead leaves, soil, and silk. It is attached on one side of the burrow with a silky hinge. The spider waits underneath for prey to come by. Then the door pops open. Dinner is served!

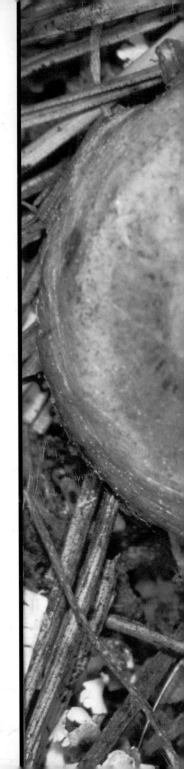

trap-door spider

21

GLOSSARY

bristle (BRISS-uhl)—short, stiff hair

burrow (BUHR-oh)—to dig a tunnel or hole in the ground; a burrow can also be a hole in the ground that an animal makes

chamber (CHAYM-buhr)—a room or enclosed space

colony (KAH-luh-nee)—a group of the same kind of animal

decomposer (dee-kuhm-PO-zur)—a living thing that turns dead things into food for others

fertilize (FUHR-tuh-lyz)—to make soil rich and healthy

grub (GRUHB)—an insect that looks like a short, white worm

invertebrate (in-VUR-tuh-bruht)—an animal without a backbone

nymph (NIMF)—a young form of an insect

prey (PRAY)—an animal that is hunted by another animal for food

silk (SILK)—a thin but strong thread made by spiders

species (SPEE-sheez)—a group of creatures that can reproduce with one another

social (SOH-shuhl)—living in groups or packs

venom (VEN-uhm)—a liquid poison made by some animals to kill prey

READ MORE

Ang, Karen. *Inside the Ants' Nest*. New York: Bearport Publishing, 2014.

Carr, Aaron. *Earthworms*. New York: Av2 by Weigl, 2014.

Lunis, Natalie. *Inside the Tarantula's Burrow*. New York: Bearport Publishing, 2014.

INTERNET SITES

FactHound offers a safe, fun way to find Internet sites related to this book.
All of the sites on FactHound have been researched by our staff.

Here's all you do:

Visit *www.facthound.com*

Type in this code: 9781491450611

Check out projects, games and lots more at
www.capstonekids.com

CRITICAL THINKING USING THE COMMON CORE

1. Reread the section about earthworms on page 6. How might the soil be different if earthworms didn't exist? Would the soil be better or worse? (Integration of Knowledge and Ideas)

2. Why do termites and ants live underground in such large groups? (Key Idea and Details)

3. Compare and contrast the tarantula discussed on page 18 with the trap-door spider discussed on page 20. How are the ways they catch prey different from one another? (Craft and Structure)

INDEX